4 4 10/18

APOSTROPHE CATASTROPHE

AND OTHER GRAMMATICAL GRUMBLES

PATRICK C. NOTCHTREE

Also by Patrick C. Notchtree
The Clouds Still Hang

This book is derived from
www.dreaded-apostrophe.com

First published 2015

The History Press
The Mill, Brimscombe Port
Stroud, Gloucestershire, GL5 2QG
www.thehistorypress.co.uk

British Library Cataloguing in Publication Data.
A catalogue record for this book is available from the British Library.

ISBN 978 0 7509 6512 5

Typesetting and origination by The History Press
Printed and bound in Malta, by Melita Press

CONTENTS

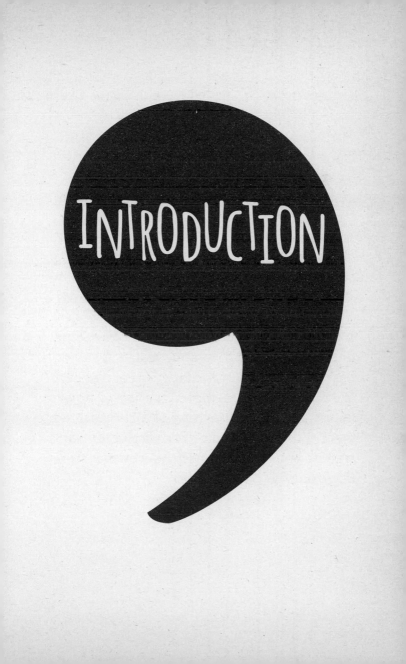

INTRODUCTION

They cause arguments. They go missing when they should be there, and they litter the place when they shouldn't. Market traders — greengrocers especially — are renowned for flinging them about with careless abandon. Some people want to ban them altogether. Others go to the extremes of pedantry in trying to keep them. Almost everybody makes them much more complicated than they need to be.

Apostrophes. Puzzled by them? Frustrated by them? Frightened of them, even? Worry not, because all is about to be revealed. By going back to the roots of the language and understanding why we use those little things, all will be made clear, and instead of a complicated system of varying rules for varying circumstances, you will realise from now on that there is just one rule. Yes, just one.

The apostrophe must be the most misunderstood and misused piece of punctuation in the English language. This is worsened by the fact that most people simply fail to understand what it does, and make it unnecessarily complicated. The result is that many people, in an effort to appear correct, use a scattergun approach, dropping in apostrophes every time the letter 's' ends a word – for plurals, possessives and contractions alike.

In fact, using the apostrophe correctly is easy – once you know the rule.

Notice I say 'the' rule. Despite the confusion about this and many variations, there is, in fact, just one place where an apostrophe is used. **Just one**. It really is easy to remember:

Use an apostrophe when letters are missing.

I have taught many children, mainly Year 6 (aged 10–11), this method over many years and 90 per cent of them have 'got it' immediately and never get it wrong again.

Explaining something in written form is not the same as interactive teaching, where the listeners respond and the teacher can adapt as they go along. I have tried to take this step by step and cover all the angles, but it means there is a lot of reading to do. Please be patient.

Darlington Memorial NHS Trust

Pay and Display Charges

1 HOUR	£1.00
2 HOUR'S	£1.30
3 HOUR'S	£2.00
4 HOUR'S	£2.50
4-24 HOUR'S	£3.00

© www.dreaded-apostrophe.com

Those of you who were taught a multi-rule method (presumably unsuccessfully or why would you be here?) are probably now puzzled. How can there be just one rule which covers all uses of the dreaded apostrophe? I repeat:

Use an apostrophe when letters are missing.

Misuse often occurs where plurals are involved. Plural simply means more than one. So we see the famous greengrocer signs like:

Carrot's cheap today

But there is nothing missing here – it just means more than one carrot – so it should read:

Carrots cheap today

Another example:

Parent's are asked to supervise their children

Again, nothing is missing; it is a request to more than one parent to look after their kids. The correct form is:

Parents are asked to supervise their children

But the children belong to the parents, you say. True, no doubt, but the two words are not together in the sentence and the message is directed at parents, not children. *Parents children* would need an apostrophe – but before or after the 's'? Have no fear, all will be explained later.

So where do we use an apostrophe?

We use an apostrophe when letters are missing.

I will look at the obvious cases first. These are where we deliberately shorten a word or phrase and then use an apostrophe to show that letters are missing.

These are called **contractions**.

In full	Letters missing	Shortened form
can not	no	can't
could not	o	couldn't
do not	o	don't
I am	a	I'm
it has	ha	it's
it is	i	it's
let us	u	let's
that is	i	that's
they are	a	they're
they had	ha	they'd
was not	o	wasn't
we had	ha	we'd
what is	i	what's
would not	o	wouldn't
you are	a	you're
you would	woul	you'd

my car is there	i	my car's there
the coat is on the peg	i	the coat's on the peg

The list above does not contain every possible abbreviated form, but from that one can see how the apostrophe goes in place of the missing letters. Missing spaces do **not** get an apostrophe. Think of it this way: it was a space so there was nothing to go missing in the first place.

People often confuse *you're* and *your*. But now you know the rule, you need never confuse them again. *You're* is short for *You are*, while *your* means belonging to you, as in 'Your head is probably spinning by now'.

© www.dreaded-apostrophe.com

There, *their* and *they're* are often confused but *there* is a place, *their* means belonging to them and *they're* is short for *they are*.

English is a living language, and all such languages contain irregularities. One which is relevant to apostrophe usage is *it's* and *its*. *It's* is short for *it is* or *it has* as you see in the table above. *Its* means belonging to *it*, as in 'It's probably spun off its neck by now'. If you are uncertain which to use, say it in full, e.g. 'The world spins on it is axis' is plainly silly, so one should use *its* rather than *it's*.

Contractions – the shortening of words and phrases – is a common use of the apostrophe to show where letters have been left out. Most people get that and understand it fairly well. A lot of the confusion arises of the use of the dreaded apostrophe to show belonging, possession and similar relationships.

I have mentioned belonging already. So what about possessives? **It is in fact the same rule.**

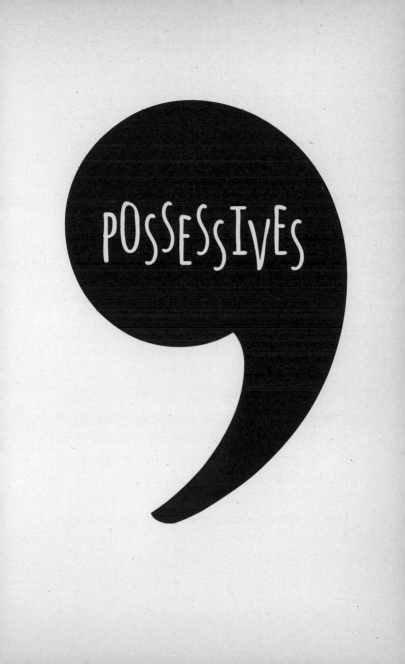
POSSESSIVES

PLURAL INITIALS

How often have you seen signs that say *CD's for sale* or similar? The *MP's voted against the bill* is another example.

These are plurals, nothing is missing, so the correct form is *CDs* and *MPs*. If your child writes that he or she gained four As at A level, be pleased also that he or she knows when *not* use an apostrophe. If they tell you they got four A's, I just hope English was not one of them!

This is by far where most of the confusion arises. Panic sets in as people think, 'Where shall I put the dreaded apostrophe?' But there is no need to panic. Keep calm; it's only an apostrophe. The same rule applies:

Use an apostrophe when letters are missing.

First, though, a little definition for readers for whom some time has passed since they were taught grammar, if at all. When we talk about nouns, these are the names of things, objects, etc. *Table*, *dog*, *coat*, *child* – these are all **nouns**. They don't have to be physical objects – *dream*, *idea*, *thought* are also nouns.

There are also **pronouns** – words that stand in for nouns: *he*, *she*, *they*, *it*. Each of these has a possessive form: *his*, *her*, *their* and *its*. That last one causes a lot of confusion, but more about *its* and *it's* later.

Other types of word are **verbs**, which are actions such as *walk, run, think,* often called 'doing words'.

Nouns and verbs can be modified or described. **Adjectives** are words that describe nouns: *big* table, *small* dog, *black* coat, *noisy* child, *bad* dream, *good* idea, *clever* thought and so on. **Adverbs** are words that describe verbs and often end in *ly*: walk *slowly*, run *quickly*, think *carefully*. I include these for the sake of completeness but adverbs don't usually cause a problem when it comes to apostrophes.

© www.dreaded-apostrophe.com

There is a class of nouns called **Proper Nouns**. Note I've used capital letters. This is because these are the names of people and places, etc. and so have capital letters; *London*, *Stephen*, *America*, *Susan*, *Titanic*, *Seattle*, *Melbourne* and so on. Notice *Titanic* got in there. The word 'ship' is a noun but ships usually have names, and those names are Proper Nouns, hence *Titanic*, *Nautilus* and so on.

Nouns can be singular or plural. Singular means there is just one: *girl*, *boy*, *ship*, *coat*. If we are writing about more than one of these

– *girls*, *boys*, *ships*, *coats* – this is the plural form. Nothing is missing here so no apostrophe is needed. Adding the letter *s* is the most common way to make a noun plural in English. Some nouns remain the same in the plural form – *sheep*, *deer* for example. Others have plural forms going back to the roots of modern English, such as child of which the plural is *children*. But these different forms do not affect the way in which we use the dreaded apostrophe to show possession. It's still the same rule:

Use an apostrophe when letters are missing.

To understand this, we need first to take a trip back in time ...

THE OLDEN DAYS

English is an old language, but an ever-changing one. Many people today find the English of Shakespeare hard to understand, but it is actually relatively modern in structure compared with English from earlier periods. It is to these earlier periods of English we must look for the roots of modern apostrophe usage.

I am also going to simplify matters, and having studied linguistics I know this may be oversimplification for some. But here the aim is to explain the dreaded apostrophe, not teach linguistics and Old or Middle English. So bear with me.

© www.dreaded-apostrophe.com

English, along with Dutch, Danish, Norwegian, Swedish, etc., is a Germanic language. It shares much in common with modern German, although a lot of vocabulary was later imported from French/Latin. Quick example: the German for foot is Fuss, for ball is Ball, so football is Fussball. (Note that in German, **all** nouns have a capital letter, not just Proper Nouns.) We get the word 'pedestrian' from the French/Latin side though. Some Germanic usage survives in English, particularly in North American English where some archaic forms remain in use – gotten for instance. The -*en* participle ending will be familiar to German speakers.

A simple sentence such as *The girl catches the ball* has a **subject**, a **verb** and an **object**. We have already learnt that a verb is a 'doing' word and a noun is the name of a 'thing'. In a sentence, a noun can be a subject or an object. The **subject** in a sentence (in this case *The girl*) is the noun 'doing' the verb, in this case, the catching. The **object** is the noun which is having something done to it, in this case, being caught, which is the ball. So:

| The girl | catches | the ball. |
| **Subject** | **Verb** | **Object** |

or

| Bill | cooked | supper. |
| **Subject** | **Verb** | **Object** |

They are not always in this order, for example the sentence below:

| The child | (was) bitten | (by a) dog. |
| **Object** | **Verb** | **Subject** |

As the dog is doing the biting and the child is being bitten, the dog is the subject and the child is the object.

So you can see that different words have different jobs to do in a sentence.

In German, nouns follow a **case** system. This is a system of changes or modifications that a word undergoes depending on which job it is doing in the sentence.

© www.dreaded-apostrophe.com

© www.dreaded-apostrophe.com

Why not try one of our delicious coffee's or hot chocolate's ?

CAPPUCCINO- Hot milk with a shot of espresso and a dusting of chocolate on the top
ESPRESSO- Small shot of black coffee
COFFEE- Mug of black coffee
CAFE AU LAIT- Mug of ...
CHOCOL...

© www.dreaded-apostrophe.com

For example, in German the subject of the sentence is in the **nominative** case and the object of the sentence is in the **accusative** case. As we have seen, in the simple sentence, *The girl catches the ball.* the verb is catches. The girl is the subject of the sentence because she is doing the catching. The ball is the object of the sentence because that is what gets caught. So:

The girl	*catches*	*the ball*
Nominative Subject		Accusative Object

The case which denotes possession is called the **genitive** case. So a subject (in the example below, *the man*) which possesses something will be in the genitive case. As in:

The man's   coat
Genitive

Like German, old forms of English (which were very different to our modern language) used a genitive case ending to show possession. This was normally *-es*. For our purposes, that will do. For example, the English *The man's coat* in German is *Der Mantel des Mannes* (The coat of the man). Note the *-es* ending on *Mann* to show possession.

So now let's (let us) go back a few hundred years in English. Geoffrey Chaucer wrote his famous *Canterbury Tales* in the English of his time. What today we call 'The *Knight's Tale*' he wrote as:

Knyghtes Tale

Note the -es ending as in German to denote possession (*The tale of the knight*). He also writes about the *Kynges court* and *Goddes love*. But in modern English, of all varieties, the 'e' is missed out. Coupled with modern spelling, *Kynges court* becomes *King's court* and *Goddes love* becomes *God's love*. The old -es possessive form in English is now missing, and as I am sure you will now remember we

Use an apostrophe when letters are missing.

© www.dreaded-apostrophe.com

We can use this insight to help us place apostrophes correctly. Remember above I talked about *Parents children*. Does the apostrophe come before or after the 's'? If we pretend we are Chaucer, it becomes easy.

	Pretend Chaucer	Modern correct form
One *parent* and his or her children	*parent*es children	*parent*'s children
All *parents* and all their children	*parent*ses children	*parents*' children

In the plural we could say parents's and drop only the 'e' but having 's's' seems a bit silly here so the whole *es* goes missing to be replaced by the apostrophe, leaving parents' as the plural possessive form.

Note that this applies only to the possessive form of plural nouns. The question of possession with singular nouns that end in *s* is a different matter and is dealt with a little later.

Take *the boys coat*. Unless several boys share a coat (unlikely) we can assume this is one boy and his coat, so *the boyes coat* shortens to *the boy's coat*.

If we take *the boys coats* we are not sure now whether this is one boy with a lot of coats or lots of boys and all their coats.

	Pretend Chaucer	Modern correct form
one boy with a lot of coats	*boyes* coats	*boy's* coats
lots of boys and their coats	*boyses* coats	*boys'* coats

In the first case, we have one *boy* to which we add the -*es* to show possession, to give us *boyes*. Today, the -*e* is missing, replaced by the apostrophe to give *boy's* so the apostrophe ends up before the 's'.

In the second case, we have a plural *boys* to which we add the -*es* to show possession, to give us *boyses*, Today, the -*es* is missing, replaced by the apostrophe to give *boys'* so the apostrophe ends up after the 's'.

© www.dreaded-apostrophe.com

This example clearly shows why an apostrophe, not just included but included in the correct place, can be important. Its use and correct positioning can radically alter the meaning of what is being written.

Something that gets people confused is a word like children. (Making a plural with *-en* is another Germanic throwback.) Because they are not using the correct rule they assume that because children is plural, the apostrophe must come after the 's'. So we get childrens' which is wrong.

© www.dreaded-apostrophe.com

© www.dreaded-apostrophe.com

But my consistent system takes care of that. Think it through – take the example *childrens toys*. We can safely guess there is more than one child involved here because of the word children.

	Pretend Chaucer	Modern correct form
childrens toys	*childrenes toys*	*children's* toys

The 'e' goes missing and the apostrophe ends up correctly before the 's'.

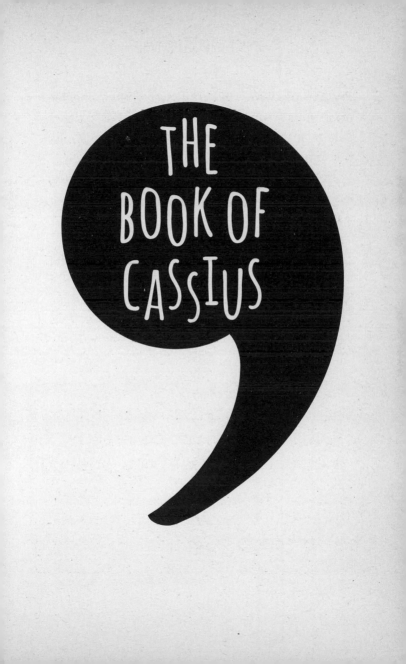

THE
BOOK OF
CASSIUS

People sometimes get confused when a singular noun ends in the letter 's'. Because of that 's', panic sets in and people wonder which rule to apply. But remember, **there is only one rule**. Use it.

In the case of a book belonging to Cassius, we will use the 'Chaucer' rule to place the apostrophe.

	Pretend Chaucer	Modern correct form
Cassiuss book	Cassiuses book	Cassius's book

| sees the first Solar Eclipse in the UK s|
ver 90% of the suns disc covered by the|
a spectacular moment and one that|

cted to reach its maximum at app|
d like all students and staff to witnes|

Just apply the rule and the apostrophe will end up in the correct place. This clearly demonstrates that Cassius is singular, i.e. there is just one Cassius we are talking about, and he possesses the book. To omit the last *s* as some do fails to make it clear there is just one Cassius. Of course, one might argue that because there is just one book, it's pretty obvious there is one Cassius. But imagine we were discussing more than one book, a library even! If in that case we were faced with *Cassius' books* the reader might have doubt as to whether the many books belonged to one Cassius or many. But applying the rule and being consistent makes it clear.

Of course, Cassius is a Proper Noun, somebody's name. But the same rule applies to ordinary nouns that end in *s*, such as actress or princess.

	Pretend Chaucer	Modern correct form
A princess with a gown	princesses gown	princess's gown
Many princesses with gowns	princesseses gowns	princesses's gowns

<u>**GYMNASTICS TIME CH**</u>

Dear Parent/Guardian
The time of you're child's gymnastics coaching

Please note as from Tuesday 2nd November 5.0
<u>**NEW TIME**</u> <u>**of 5.15pm – 6.00pm**</u>

Thank You

I think we can safely assume that the situation where several princesses share a single gown is highly unlikely.

Now we can see that there *really* is only one rule:

Use an apostrophe when letters are missing.

We have covered both **contractions** (things like *cannot* becoming *can't*) as well as **possession** (where the apostrophe stands in for the missing possessive word ending that is no longer used in modern English). And you should now even understand why, in the case of possession, it sometimes comes before the s and other times after the s.

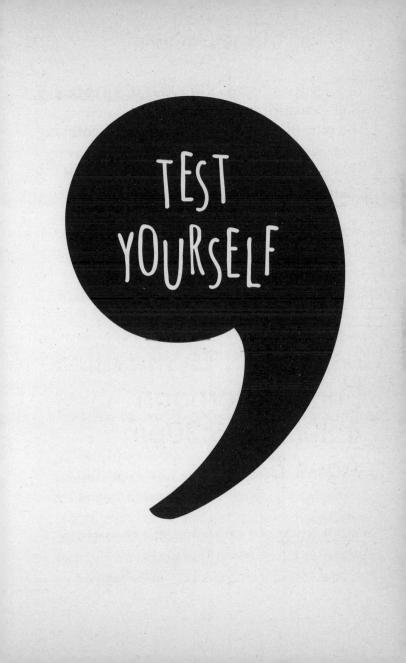

TEST YOURSELF

So why not try out your new-found knowledge?

Coming up is a little story which is designed to test the use of the dreaded apostrophe – dreaded no longer I hope. I suggest you use a pencil – then you can try it out on friends and family as well. I am not going to mark it – you're grown up enough to have got this far so you can mark your own. (Note the use of *you're* and *your* in that sentence.)

Good luck.

Beginners Gymnastics
Friday afternoon
4:30pm – 5:30pm
Ages 5+

For more information or to book a place on one of the sessions simply ask at reception

THE SHOPPING TRIP

The boys and girls decided to go to town for a look round because there wasnt much to do at home. Johns coat was torn, so he borrowed his sisters. She wasnt going with them.

'Lets go round the shops,' said Susans brother, Stephen. The childrens parents had given them some money to spend.

'Dont you lose it,' Richards father had said to him, so Richards money was in his pocket when he set out, but Alans had a zIp so he ended up carrying Richards money as well as his own so they couldnt lose it.

In the shop, Alans zip got stuck, but Lucys skill got it open again.

'Thats good,' said Alan, 'both Richards and my moneys in there. Now its OK and we cant get into trouble.'

The boys money was more than the girls, but theyd decided to share it equally. Then some of the boys said they wouldnt share it and the girls said theyd broken the agreement.

'Share it out,' said Anne. 'Its what you said youd do!'

'No, cant,' said David.

'Perhaps wed better,' said Richard, 'Its what we said wed do.'

'OK,' said David, 'I expect youre right but Im not very happy.'

The boys money and the girls money was all put in Johns coat pocket because none of the girls coat pockets were deep enough.

The childrens afternoon was spent looking round, but they couldnt find anything they wanted to buy, so, in the end, the boys and girls went off to their homes.

'Wow!' said Johns sister. 'Whats all this money doing in my coat pocket? Im rich!'

Well, did you cheat? Time now to check your answers.

THE SHOPPING TRIP

The boys and girls decided to go to town for a look round because there <u>wasn't</u> much to do at home. <u>John's</u> coat was torn, so he borrowed his sister's. She <u>wasn't</u> going with them.

'<u>Let's</u> go round the shops,' said <u>Susan's</u> brother, Stephen. The <u>children's</u> parents had given them some money to spend.

'<u>Don't</u> you lose it,' <u>Richard's</u> father had said to him, so <u>Richard's</u> money was in his pocket when he set out, but <u>Alan's</u> had a zip so he ended up carrying <u>Richard's</u> money as well as his own so they <u>couldn't</u> lose it.

In the shop, <u>Alan's</u> zip got stuck, but <u>Lucy's</u> skill got it open again.

'<u>That's</u> good,' said Alan, 'both <u>Richard's</u> and my <u>money's</u> in there. Now <u>it's</u> OK and we <u>can't</u> get into trouble.'

The <u>boys'</u> money was more than the <u>girls'</u>, but <u>they'd</u> decided to share it equally. Then some of the boys said they <u>wouldn't</u> share it and the girls said <u>they'd</u> broken the agreement.

'Share it out,' said Anne. '<u>It's</u> what you said <u>you'd</u> do!'

'No, <u>can't</u>,' said David.

'Perhaps <u>we'd</u> better,' said Richard, '<u>It's</u> what we said <u>we'd</u> do.'

'OK,' said David, 'I expect <u>you're</u> right but <u>I'm</u> not very happy.'

The <u>boys'</u> money and the <u>girls'</u> money was all put in <u>John's</u> coat pocket because none of the <u>girls'</u> coat pockets were deep enough.

The <u>children's</u> afternoon was spent looking round, but they <u>couldn't</u> find anything they wanted to buy, so, in the end, the boys and girls went off to their homes.

'Wow!' said <u>John's</u> sister. '<u>What's</u> all this money doing in my coat pocket? <u>I'm</u> rich!'

I have underlined all the missing apostrophes in the text. When I was writing it, I laid a few traps as well, with a scattering of plurals that might have tempted you. So if you put an apostrophe in where it's not underlined here then I'm afraid you've fallen headlong into one of those traps. Have a look back and see if you can work out why that word does not need an apostrophe. Conversely, if you haven't, then look back and see if you can work out why you missed it.

SOME OTHER GRAMMATICAL GRUMBLES

The reader will have realised by now that the author is a fully paid-up, card-carrying pedant. While this book and my website is focussed primarily on the use of the dreaded apostrophe – and disseminates the single-rule system for that – no piece of pedantry on this scale would be complete without mentioning some of the other grammatical errors that jar and scrape in my and other pedants' minds when seen or heard.

© www.dreaded-apostrophe.com

The English language has evolved over centuries to its present state and of course continues to evolve, both in vocabulary and grammatical usage. Just fifty years ago, when I was a lad, if somebody had said *internet* or *wifi* to me it would have meant nothing. Even a computer was generally referred to as an 'electronic brain' and they were to be a little feared. A television series like *A for Andromeda* didn't help!

© www.dreaded-apostrophe.com

English is a hard language to learn
Native English speakers love to think this, pointing out some oddities of spelling such as the many ways of pronouncing *ough*. In fact, this is not true. English has some oddities, it's true, but so do all languages. Some, like Russian and German are very phonetic and the *ough* type of question doesn't arise. But the complexities of German grammar are far more complex than English. In German the main declension allows for sixteen possible noun variations, depending on gender, case and plurality. On top of that, the adjectives all have to 'agree' with their noun and native German speakers argue about this too.

English has mercifully abandoned case endings in most situations. The genitive case apostrophe has survived because it fulfils an essential function as I hope these pages have made clear. So those learning English don't have to worry about case endings.

Neither do they have to be concerned with gender. Those learning German have to cope with three genders: masculine, feminine and neuter. But these aren't allocated logically. A girl, for example, is neuter, because all words ending in *chen* are neuter. French has masculine and feminine, but I've never yet discovered why a table is masculine in German but feminine in French. A remnant in English is calling ships and some other things *she*. But nobody would mind if you said *it* of a ship.

And despite *ough*, English is largely phonetic (or, more accurately, phonemic, but there's not the space here to start on phonemes) – if pronounced correctly. More so, I suggest, than French for example, which has more silent letters than English – until they start to sing, that is.

As languages go, English is relatively easy to learn. It is reasonably simple in structure and lacks some of the complexities of other languages. It is also a very rich language, with a large vocabulary enabling nuances of meaning not available in some others – also not available to many native speakers whose vocabulary is often more restricted. These are among the reasons why it is such a successful language and is spoken worldwide, and is often the common language when people from many countries meet for conferences, etc. Of course the extent of the British Empire helped and this

© www.dreaded-apostrophe.com

© www.dreaded-apostrophe.com

was continued when the United States succeeded Britain as the world's superpower. In the late nineteenth century, the first German Chancellor, Otto von Bismarck, said, 'The most important single political fact for at least the next 100 years is that the British and Americans speak the same language.' He wasn't wrong.

Less and fewer

It really grates when I hear people use *less* when they should be saying *fewer*. To go back to the unfortunate greengrocer who might say, 'We've got less carrots today' when he should be saying *fewer* carrots. It's actually quite simple: if the noun is singular then use *less*. If the noun is plural, use *fewer*. So there may be fewer carrots today, and that means there will be less carrot cake. I find that fewer children like carrots than chocolate.

Following the rule *less with a singular noun and fewer with a plural noun* will serve you right at least 99 per cent of the time.

© www.dreaded-apostrophe.com

Of and have

This horrendous error has crept in more in recent years and is a result of poor speech. *I would of gone if I had the money. You should of given it to me.* Ouch!

Of is a very useful little preposition and is used in all sorts of ways quite correctly. But it is NEVER a verb. Not even a verb participle. In the horrible sentence above, *of* is being used mistakenly instead of *have*. The verb 'to have' is used in participle mode to form various verb tenses, such as the past perfect tense and as above in conditional mode. The correct version is:

I would have gone if I had the money. You should have given it to me.

Of course, using the dreaded apostrophe, this becomes:

I would've gone if I had the money. You should've given it to me.

Then people with poor diction go on to say it as *should of* and then they write it as such.

No doubt somebody as curious about grammar as you, dear reader, would never make such an error!

Very unique

If something is unique, it means it is the only one. That's it – just one. It cannot be more unique than unique. It cannot be very unique because there can be no degrees of uniqueness. It's either unique or it's not.

Advise, advice, practise and practice
People often confuse these. But the -*ise* words are verbs and the -*ice* words are nouns. So one may have 'I advise you to take my advice'. That is easier because the words are pronounced differently with the -*ise* ending being softer than the -*ice* ending. That can't be used to remind one which is which when it comes to practise and practice, as they are both said the same way. But if you remember that advise is a verb it will remind you that practise is a verb. 'I need to practise my piano playing more.' 'I must do more piano practice.'

Affect and effect
This is another case of a verb and noun causing confusion. Affect is the verb. Once something has been affected, it may show the effect. Many people pronounce the two words the same way but that is poor practice. My view is that they should be pronounced slightly differently, as **a**ffect and **e**ffect. Again, poor diction leads to errors.

Much less commonly, effect can be used as a verb in certain circumstances. This is when an action intends to cause change, such as 'The campaigners were trying to effect a change in the way we think.'

Only

This is often placed incorrectly in a sentence. Consider these two sentences:

I only *drive on weekends.*

I drive only *on weekends.*

While logic tells you that in the first case the speaker uses their car at weekends but not during the week, in fact it means that the speaker does no other activity at weekends apart from driving. No sleeping, no eating, etc. Just driving.

The second sentence makes it clear that driving is restricted to weekends but not to the exclusion of all other activities.

You may be thinking the meaning is obvious and this is pedantry taken to the extreme. Normally this might be so, but lawyers would have a field day over that kind of difference!

FREQUENTLY ASKED QUESTIONS

Not very long after my website first went online some years ago, I started to receive requests for help and clarification. I have done my best to help and I think by and large I have. I have even been called an angel, and told that my correspondent is in love with me! Hyperbole I'm sure, but the sentiment is appreciated. I have also been assumed to be a 40-year-old lady librarian. I'm not.

© www.broadsheet.ie

I have no doubt that the reader of this book will also have questions and you may well find it has been asked before and that the answer here. One would think that after several years every question about apostrophes would have been asked, and I think most possibilities are covered in these FAQ pages. The questions keep coming though, and many have raised interesting topics and led to some fascinating discussions

You may find what appear to be inconsistencies and variations in what seem to be the same problem. In my defence all I can say is that on each occasions I try to look at each problems in its own context and answer as best I can. Also, although I talk a lot about the single 'rule', I am not using the word rule in some kind of grammatical legal sense. As far as I'm aware there is no legislation in any jurisdiction that lays down rules for the English language. That is one of the reasons for its success as a language; it is dynamic, growing and ever changing. That's not to say there isn't good practice and no standards of literacy that should be maintained. But the guiding principle should be clarity of communication and lack of ambiguity.

This section contains the Q&As of a general nature or where it is hard to classify the nature of the question being asked. Where a questioner has a query that covers more than one category it might also be included in this general category, or placed where the principal or more interesting question would indicate. In order to help the reader find the answer to a specific topic, further sections of Q&A follow gathered, I hope, into logical groups.

I encourage the reader to browse through the various Q&A sections as some of the discussions are quite enlightening, both about the confusion the little apostrophe can cause and the solutions to the problems that arise. I hope that these will add to the reader's understanding of the dreaded apostrophe.

,

Q: I am a Year 3 teacher. Please help clarify an amiable dispute between a colleague and myself. How would you HANDwrite contractions such as:

don't; couldn't

I think you would join the don, leave a gap, then write the t, then put the apostrophe in the gap. My colleague insists that you would write the *do*, leave a small gap, then the *nt* written together, with the apostrophe just between them.

Your advice would be much appreciated.

A: Well, this is a handwriting issue more than a grammatical one, especially as you both agree where the apostrophe should be.

I'm on your side here, although I can see your colleague's reasoning. Although *don't* is a contraction of *do not* it is established as a single 'word' and if it is never printed with a gap why would one want to make a difference when writing it? Does your colleague type it with a gap? If not, why is he or she inconsistent in this respect? How does he or she actually say it? With a small gap? :-)

I have never tried my method with Year 3, but it does work with Year 5 and especially Year 6.

,

Q: Here at the Glasgow Centre for Population Health (where the three of us discussing this

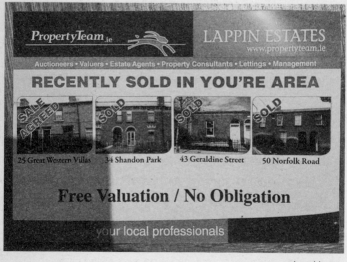

PropertyTeam.ie

LAPPIN ESTATES
www.propertyteam.ie

Auctioneers • Valuers • Estate Agents • Property Consultants • Lettings • Management

RECENTLY SOLD IN YOU'RE AREA

SALE AGREED — 25 Great Western Villas

SOLD — 34 Shandon Park

SOLD — 43 Geraldine Street

SOLD — 50 Norfolk Road

Free Valuation / No Obligation

your local professionals

have seven degrees between us!) we are having a heated debate about the correct place for the apostrophe in a title of research. The research is considering the response of 720 unconnected individuals to external effects of stress, including psychological, biological and social. We want to know how to phrase the title of the research, please?

Is it:

Individual responses to stress and deprivation.
Individual's responses to stress and deprivation.
Individuals' responses to stress and deprivation.

We hope you can help. I have a tenner on this! :-)
Many thanks

A: It sounds like you've had enough stress in the office without bothering with a survey!

1. *Individual* responses to stress and deprivation

In this case the word *Individual* is used as an adjective to describe the responses.

What sort of responses are they? Individual responses.

2. *Individual's* responses to stress and deprivation

Here *Individual's* is a possessive, not describing the responses as such, but saying to whom the responses belong, in this case to a single individual, so a very quick survey in this case. But 720 individuals were surveyed!

3. *Individuals'* responses to stress and deprivation

Here *Individuals'* is again a possessive, not describing the responses as such, but saying to whom the responses belong, in this case to many individuals.

So, number 2 is definitely not correct as you asked 720 people. (It would be if you only asked one person and made up the other 719, but that would give the game away!)

So we come down to 1 or 3. As your survey concerns many differing responses to stress, which I assume you are going to describe, I would use number 1, the adjectival use 'Individual responses to stress and deprivation', and forget about possessives and therefore apostrophes completely.

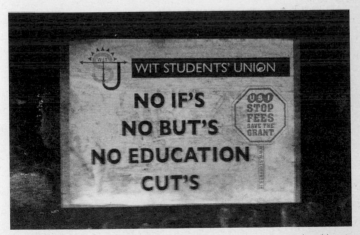

Q: In correspondence a chap referred to me as *a working mans' Lenin*.

In a fit of pique I chided him for his misuse of the apostrophe and said it should be *working man's Lenin*.

The academic help he sought agrees with him but following your simple rule I cannot see how this can be.

If I'm wrong I'll have to apologise. Do I need to?
Sincerely John, Chisholm, UK

A: In short, no. I believe you were correct.

Q: Please settle an office dispute. Which is the correct way to spell the possessive singular usage for propertys (one property) as *property's* or *propertys'*.

A: If it is one property one is talking about, then *property's* is correct: e.g. 'The property's lease has been renewed.' For more than one property, the plural is *properties*. In that case it would be '*The properties' leases have all expired.*'

UCL *Proofreaders*

CONTACT US FOR A PERSONALISED CONSULTATION

www.lessstupiderrors.com
→ FEWER

ACTUALLY I THINK IT MEANS THE SAME NUMBER OF ERRORS,
JUST ONES THAT ARE LESS STUPID

© www.broadsheet.ie

Q: I was wondering about the use of *nor* in the following phrase:

No reservation desired nor required.

Should it be *or*? Would it make more sense with a comma in front of *nor*?

A: I think either is acceptable, perhaps with a slight bias towards *nor* as it's a negative phrase. The comma is not necessary in either case.

The meaning is clear either way, and that is what language is about, after all!

,

Q: Is it true words ending in x or z do not require a possessive apostrophe?

A: No. Take for example the word fox. One fox in his lair would have a *fox's* lair. A family of foxes in their lair would have a *foxes'* lair. See the section on 'Parents children' to explain why it's not *foxes's* lair.

At this time on a Good Friday morning I am unable to think of a word ending in z, but the rule would still apply.

,

Q: I have an apostrophe question. You say use an apostrophe when something is missing. What about its use with acronyms? Clearly many letters are missing. On the Dr Grammar website he said you would not use an apostrophe for the plural form of an acronym. This makes sense with your rule.

We sell Coded Wire Tags (CWTs). Something is Coded Wired Tagged. Is this thing CWTed or CWT'ed? I guess it's the former.

A: Let's first establish a difference between an **acronym** and a set of **initials**. Your CWT example is not an acronym but initials. Purists would no doubt argue that it should be C.W.T. anyway. But the usage of full stops after initials as in U.S.A. or U.K. has reduced in recent years leading to USA and UK and in your case CWT. Initials are not words and to say CWTed is really a jargon attempting to apply standard rules to a jargon expression. Nothing wrong with that per se, it's useful shorthand for people who understand what they mean by it. Written down I would prefer CWTed to CWT'ed.

Acronyms are an attempt to create a new word from initials. Sometimes the initials lend themselves to it easily, e.g. UNESCO. Sometimes, especially in German, the first part of each word is used to abbreviate a long term into a shorter one, the most infamous example being the Secret State Police, Geheime Staats Polizei. Take the first letters of each word and you have Gestapo. It can be argued that an acronym such as Gestapo is a new word in itself, especially when imported into English, and should therefore be subject to normal grammatical rules. So 'The Gestapo's headquarters were in Prinz Albrecht Straße' requires the apostrophe because it's a possessive. Had there been several Gestapos — well, that's a plural.

,

© AnemoneProjector

Q: I wondered if I could get your opinion on the use/placement of an apostrophe in the following situation:

The borrower(s) rights must be observed.

With the possible plural of the word borrower in play, it's not clear to me whether the apostrophe should appear before or after the bracketed 's'. The easy way out, of course, would be to rewrite the sentence as:

The rights of the borrower(s) must be observed.

This is likely the approach that I'll recommend, but I did still wonder about the appropriate placement of the apostrophe in the first example. If you have insights or comments, I'd be interested in reading them.

A: It's an interesting one, and you are the first to raise it. It shows how language is dynamic and ever changing. Having the *s* in brackets shows that the writer intends to cover both singular and plural possibilities, but, of course, there would be an *s* there either way. Perhaps a more pedantically accurate rendition (but an absurd one) would be:

The borrower(')s(') rights must be observed.

indicating that the apostrophe could be either before or after the *s* depending on whether the instance was singular or plural.

Your second version is not just the easy way out. It is also sensible and, I would argue, better grammatically.

© Avi

Q: Hello, just wondering if you can clear up a dispute at the office. Which of the below would be a proper use of the apostrophe?

1. *I have both my client's authority.*
2. *I have both my clients' authority.*

A: There is a more at issue here than the apostrophe. Given that one is talking about two clients, each of whom can give authority, then we have more than one client and more than one authority. So strictly speaking it should be: *I have both my clients' authorities.*

But that may seem over pedantic so one could rephrase the whole thing and use *authority* in a generic sense as in

I have authority from both my clients.

If you don't wish to go as far as that, I suggest you use your version 2 above.

© Beth Granter

Q: Could you help with this query please?

Members are encouraged to accept each others' weaknesses as well as to celebrate each others' strengths.

Are the apostrophes in the right place in this sentence or should it read 'each other's'?
Clarification would be gratefully received.

A: The issue revolves around whether we are dealing with a singular or a plural. Because of the nature of the situation it would at first appear it is a plural, but on examination it is in fact singular. Try expressing it this way, 'Members are encouraged to accept the weaknesses of each other as well as to celebrate the strengths of each other.'

Now it can be seen that *each other* is singular and therefore the rule should be applied in that way (other otheres other's):

Members are encouraged to accept each other's weaknesses as well as to celebrate each other's strengths.

,

Q: Where, in the following sentence, does the apostrophe go?

A persons Will can help the Society in all of its work.

The word 'Will' in this case is as in Last Will and Testament.

I say there isn't one — but a colleague says there is one in 'persons' and my boss agrees. I have had them both insist and my boss explain how and why — but I still feel my English teacher smacking my wrist for putting apostrophes in places they shouldn't belong!!! That was twenty-five years ago now!!!!

Help me please!!!!! (and forgive my excessive exclamation mark usage)

A: I think your English teacher must have been a fearsome person! I am afraid that your colleague and boss are correct on this one. It is a possessive and therefore should be in the genitive (possessive) case.

Using my system:

person using 'Pretend Chaucer' becomes *per-sones* which we abbreviate to *person's*.

A person's Will can help the Society in all of its work.

Q: My friend's name is Adams. Somewhere in school, I was told the rule for possessive nouns varied depending on whether the noun was one syllable or more than one syllable. Would you write '*Adams'* life' or '*Adams's* life'?

Would the rule be the same for a one-syllable proper noun ending with 's'? My nickname is Sis, so I think one would write 'Sis's car...'.

A: Whoever told you that should have been sacked. The number of syllables is not a factor. Just apply the rule!

Q: Thank you so much for participating in this year's fair.

Do I need an apostrophe? My boss thinks I do.

A: Your boss is correct. :-)

It's *the fair of this year* and as such is in the genitive case. In old English 'Pretend Chaucer' this would therefore have had the *es* case ending, now shortened to *year's*.

© Darren Foreman

Q: *Do's and Don'ts:* I know there isn't supposed to be an apostrophe after *do*, I just can't explain why. Can you give me an explanation?

A: There is nothing missing. The addition of the *s* is to make a plural form of *do*. The problem is that grammatically speaking, only nouns can have plurals in this way, not verbs. The expression is a form of slang and is understood to mean *things that one should do and things that one should not do.* In this case *do* and *don't* are verbs being used as though they are nouns and then attempting to apply plural forms to them, so grammatical problems are inevitable. Also, simply adding *s* to *do* makes it look like an early Microsoft operating system, DOS, rather than the intended meaning.

How to express such ungrammatical vernacular forms poses problems for pedants!

Q: Do we say the *60s* or the *60's*?

A: *60s* — it's a simple plural. You need to use a possessive but the apostrophe would come after the 's':

60s' music is better than today's.

Q: I have this sentence:
What could be more embarrassing than forgetting one of our valued customer's birthdays?

Because I used one would customer's be like that? Or should it be like this: customers'?

A: Well, with luck you've only forgotten one birthday, of one customer. So the apostrophe before the *s* is correct.

Q: I'm looking everywhere for a punctuation rule. Perhaps you've come across one which would govern the following situation. The sentence in question:

He pointed at the blackberry vines. 'Start hackin'.'

Most guidebooks indicate to put the punctuation INSIDE the quotation marks like so:

'Start hackin.''

But in this case, the single marker is an apostrophe indicating a missing letter, not a single quote mark. It seems more logical to me to keep the 'word+apostrophe' together.

Yes, I know I could rewrite the sentence, but I write country, and this comes up a lot, so I might as well search for a definitive answer. Have you discovered a rule to cover this example?

A: You are right. I'm not sure what guidebooks you refer to, but ignore that, at least. The apostrophe goes where the missing letter is. To put it after the full stop is nonsense. So go with:

He pointed at the blackberry vines. 'Start hackin'.'

I hope this helps.

Q: On occasion, we hold a meeting for those women who are married to a pastor. The meeting is called *The Pastors Wives Conference*. However, it was noted that this could mean a pastor had several wives ... and you may imagine the humour this has produced!

Many heads have been scratched over this, and I hope you can help.

A: There is more than one pastor and more than one wife. So applying the rule (as in the boys and their coats) you arrive at *The Pastors' Wives' Conference*.

Q: I've got an example question about where to place the missing apostrophe which is:

Swimmers belongings must not be left at the poolside.

What I'm confused about is if the apostrophe goes before or after the 's' because it is obviously talking about more than one swimmer.

A: Think about 'lots of boys and their coats' in relation to lots of swimmers and their belongings. Let me know what you think.

Q: So you're saying that the sentence should be:

Swimmers' belongings must not be left at the poolside. ?

A: You have it correct.

Q: I wonder if you could help me with an invitation I'm sending. It reads:

Mandy and Ricky present
A Wilde Summer's Ball
Enjoy a wonderful summers evening, etc., etc.

Could you please settle a dispute over whether both *Summers* have apostrophes or just one.
  Kind regards

A: In your case, both need the apostrophe, before the 's'. Or you could omit the 's' and use *Summer Ball* in which case *Summer* becomes an adjective describing the ball.

Is there a reason for spelling wild with an 'e' on the end? Unless it's your surname of course.

R: Of course I was right and my husband was wrong. Wilde is our surname.

© Eric E. Castro

Q: Can you help please? Where does the apostrophe go in:

There were

A: It doesn't. :)

,

Q: I'm wondering whether you had a view on the position below, which is causing quite a bit of debate at our office.

We have set up a framework of ten contractors. In essence we set up the framework and the contractors are classed as being 'on the framework'. The framework is called the *Contractors Framework*. Debate rages as to whether it should have an apostrophe after the 's' to read '*Contractors' Framework*' or whether it is simply '*Contractors Framework*'? Does the issue hinge on who owns the framework? Are there any rules on this as we set up the framework it can be argued it is ours but we as an organisation are not on the framework but did set it up and manage it. Therefore, is possession of the framework with the contractors suggesting that the apostrophe should come after the 's'?

A: Try not to take possession too literally. It is a framework for multiple contractors and so I would suggest *Contractors' Framework.*

© Frank Hebbert

Q: I can't get my head around the following ...

The changing room for boys

Is it:
The boys changing room
or
The boys' changing room?

It doesn't belong to the boys. The teacher at my son's school seems to suggest that it should be *The boy's changing room*. But I can't see that that is correct.
　The other one was:

The football team for girls

The girls football team
or
The girls' football team?

Any help appreciated. Thank you.

A: No, but it's a changing room for boys. Don't take possession too literally. The teacher is only correct if it is a changing room for just one boy. Unlikely. Change schools if that's their standard: *Boys' changing room*.

A team by definition implies more than one girl: *Girls' football team*.

Q: Hello. *Seniors' Section* is used in the *Seniors' Section Rules* of my club and that I believe to be correct. Similarly for *Seniors' Captain*, etc. However, we have the *Current Senior's Captain* and three previous *Senior's Captains* and I believe this use to be incorrect because it is his title and therefore does not require an apostrophe. Advice welcome!

A: Assuming there is more than one senior, all occurrences should have the apostrophe after the 's'.

© James O. Gorman

Q: I am still unclear on my particular issue:

artist's group
or
artists' group

There are several artists, only one group. In your 'boy's coat' example there are many boys with many coats, or one boy with one coat, but not as here, many boys with one coat! So as far as

I can see, my example is subtly different from the examples on your pages.

My guess would be *artists'*.

Can you advise!

Many thanks – Chuck

A: Your guess is correct because it is a group for more than one artist.

Q: Would it be correct to say *Joshua's school*. When Joshua does not posses the school, but is part of it? I look forward to your thoughts.

A: Please don't take possession too literally. He doesn't have to own the school to be a part of it, for it to be 'his' school. *Joshua's school* is correct.

© JD

Q: I'm stuck with a singular noun that ends in 'X'. If something belonged to said noun, where would the dreaded apostrophe go?
e.g. A hammer that belongs to a toolbox:

The toolbox's hammer – this looks correct to me, but nothing is missing ...
The toolboxes' hammer – this looks incorrect to me

A: Just follow the rule:

box + pretend Chaucer = boxes. Drop the 'e' = box's

Q: Could you advise me if it is *loves, love's* or *loves'* as in *'mummy loves you'*. I'm pretty sure it's loves but I'm not certain, please can you help me?

A: It is simply the second-person form of the verb 'to love'. So no apostrophe is needed.

Q: Which is correct:

One thinks again.
or
One think's again ?

A: The first one. It is neither a contraction nor possession. Verbs cannot possess.

Q: I am a proofreader for an author of railway books and at times I feel that World War Three has broken out by virtue of his refusal to accept some of my corrections. The latest were sentences that contained references to the *Crossing Keepers Hut* and to the *Butchers shop*. I had corrected these to the *Crossing Keeper's Hut* and to the *Butcher's shop*. In both cases I had assumed that the hut and the shop related to just one person and not two or more when the apostrophe would have followed the letter 's'. In both cases my correction was rejected by his simple statement of 'Not now'. He maintains that in the modern world we don't use the apostrophe in these words any more, but I feel he is wrong.

What are your views please?

Railway trains usually have a person in charge of the train called a guard. They usually have a separate section of the train in which they sit and this is usually referred to as the *Guards Van*, or should it be *Guard's Van*? Is this one of those instances where there is an exception to the rule and the word guard has become adjectival?

You might like to also comment on another difference of opinion between us although not relating to apostrophes, one that he will just not budge on, and that is the word *nor*. He states that it old fashioned and no one uses it any more. I would certainly agree that it is not used as often as it should, but would hardly agree that it is old fashioned as it has a totally different meaning to *or*. He states that 'The station had no goods or parcels office.' To me, this indicates that it was missing one of them, but he is unsure of which one as the use of the word *or* gives a choice. I say it should be 'The station had no goods nor parcels office' which clearly indicates that both were absent, but he won't have it. If you see a notice that states 'No Cycling nor Horse Riding' then you know that both are banned, but if the notice reads 'No Cycling or Horse Riding' then this gives one a choice of which one not to do. Obviously this is not what the council who put up the notice intended, but it is the true interpretation and would certainly make a useful legal argument should you ever find yourself in a court of law.

A: All I can say is that I agree with you on every count. But I wouldn't try using it as a legal defence! Stick to your guns!

© Jeffrey Beall

Q: Good afternoon. Can you please tell me which is the correct grammar in the following two sentences, and why? They refer to a film:

1. *The Dead Poets' Society.*
or
2. *The Dead Poets Society.*

I say that it should be 1 as the society 'belongs' to the poets, even if they are dead. If I am correct would the following sentence be correct without the apostrophe?

3. *The Dead Poets Statue.*

I suggest that the apostrophe isn't required as the statue (if there is one) doesn't 'belong' to the poets.

A: It's a society about dead poets, and I am assuming we are talking about more than one poet. When discussing possession in terms of apostrophe usage, it is used rather loosely and does not require actual ownership but more a connection. The society doesn't belong to the poets, rather the use of the term poets here is adjectival, describing the society, so I suggest no apostrophe is required.

Q: Could you explain why 'my family's keeper' is grammatically correct as opposed to 'my families keeper'? My friends and I are in the middle of a heated argument because they believe 'my families keeper' is correct, and that any grammar errors can be fixed by putting an apostrophe on the end of families.

A: It depends on how many families you have. Assuming just one, then the word is *family*. Because the family possesses a keeper, the possessive is *family's keeper*. If there are several families sharing the same keeper, then you would need *families' keeper*.

© Lungstruck

Q: *Changing family's lives*
or
Changing families' lives?

Thank you for your help.

A: Assuming it refers to more than one family, we start with the plural, *families*. Then to make it possessive we add the genitive ending to get *familieses*. Next, drop the *es* to leave us with the modern form of *families'*.

Q: I'm wondering if you can answer this question. Should an apostrophe be used below, after the 's' in Girls?

Girls Road Trip

(Should it read: *Girls' Road Trip*?)

A: It is the trip of more than one girl so *Girls' Road Trip* is correct.

Q: If a road sign says NO HGV'S is that to do with the missing letters, I can't believe it is.

A: The only explanation is that the signwriter hasn't read this book!

© Mark Roy

Q: Please will you place the apostrophe correctly in the following:

Breaking of the Print Unions power when there is more than one union involved.

A: One union – *union's*. More than one – *unions'*.

Q: I am an English woman teaching English as a second language in Spain. One of my students asked me about apostrophes, and showed me an example in a well-known textbook teaching English as a second language. The example was this:

I never buy meat at the butcher's.

I have never come across an example like this, and said I would investigate. I found your site, but I couldn't find specific examples. The only thing I can think of is that the sentence should be: I never buy meat at the butcher's shop, making it a possessive apostrophe. Am I right?

A: I think you are right. The word *shop* is implied at the end of the sentence and so *butcher's* requires the apostrophe. A less controversial alternative might be *I never buy meat at the butcher.*

Q: I received an invoice this morning from a Mr Williams, who recently did some fencing for me. Of course, he used the word *fence's*.

He's a particularly nice man, so I'm not going to scan the actual invoice for your gallery, but what blew me away completely – a thing I'd never seen before – is that he put an apostrophe in his own name! Yes, he's signed the invoice *David William's*. Is that the ultimate apostrophe?

A: As you say, that takes some beating!

Q: I'm an editor for an English magazine in Taiwan. We recently had an article titled '*A Book Lovers' Paradise*'.

I felt that it should be '*A Book Lover's Paradise*', and all the Internet articles I found with a Google search seemed to use that style. One of the other editors said that it's 'a paradise, enjoyed by numerous book lovers' (the article was about a really nice bookstore in Argentina), and therefore *Book Lovers'* was correct.

I'm still not sure, as the use of the indefinite article is complicating the issue. I'm happy with *Book Lovers' Paradise*, for example.

A: I agree that the use of the indefinite article is ambiguous. Is it a paradise for all book lovers or a paradise that a book lover will like?

There are arguments in favour of either, but I lean – just – towards it being a paradise for book lovers, so favour *A Book Lovers' Paradise*. But I would hesitate to criticise the other point of view.

Sorry I can't be more definitive. Such is the English language!

,

Q: Is the use of a double possessive correct or not? For example: *I live around the corner from a cousin of John's*. Surely this should read: *I live around the corner from a cousin of John*.

A: The latter is correct. But why not just say *John's cousin*?

© Ogeld

Q: I seem to remember my teacher saying that if I start a sentence, but leave out the first word, then an apostrophe is correct, for example:

'Hope you are well.
instead of
I hope you are well.

Can you confirm if this is right?

A: I think such usage is now so antiquated I wouldn't bother. If you are simply writing down what a person actually says, there would be no need because they didn't say *I* at the beginning of the sentence anyway.

Q: I am wondering which of these is correct:

Enjoy your favourite nights out for less.
or
Enjoy your favourite nights' out for less.

Many thanks in advance for your help!

A: The first. It is just the plural of *night*.

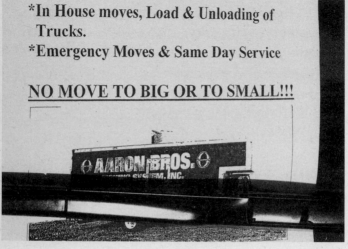

*In House moves, Load & Unloading of Trucks.
*Emergency Moves & Same Day Service

NO MOVE TO BIG OR TO SMALL!!!

© Quinn Dombrowski

Q: Can you please answer a query for me and an entire office full of frustrated apostrophe users? We are constantly being corrected by an old fossil of a stickler on the following formulation (contested apostrophe in brackets): *Upon the Mother's legal advisors(') being urged to expedite the negotiations ...*

We understand that it is not due to a missing letter and it is not possessive. My personal hunch is that it has something to do with a fossil genitive, possibly due to conjuncting a sentence using *upon*. I have also noticed the same formulation with *of*, e.g. *As a result of (my) being informed that ...*

a) Is this formulation correct?
b) Why?

A: This is a difficult one and you are the first to raise it. In your construction *being* is a gerund, basically a verb acting like a noun. In your phrase *being urged to expedite the negotiations* it acts as a verb but the phrase as a whole acts as a noun. It is therefore liable to be modified for example by a possessive pronoun as in your second example using *my*.

I have to say then in that case technically your stickler is correct. As *being urged to expedite the negotiations* is in effect a noun, it can be modified by *advisors*, which is a plural in the genitive case.

Common usage does not always follow what is technically correct, however, and many people would omit the apostrophe and not draw comment.

Personally it is not a construction I favour and I would be tempted to rewrite the whole thing perhaps along the lines, *After the mother's legal advisors were urged to expedite the negotiations* ... or similar, depending on the context.

If you decided to treat *being* as a verb form however, then this becomes an action of the advisers, in which case *advisers* is simply a plural noun and requires no apostrophe.

Q: Do we know why it is the genitive though? Does it depend on the conjunction?

A: No. It depends on 'possession', viewed in the broadest terms, not necessarily in the physical sense.

,

Less napkins. More plants. More planet.

© Redspotted

Q: I am producing some menu cards for an event run by and for the Royal Military Police Cyprus Veterans who are known, for brevity, as the RMP Cyprus Veterans Group.

Should my heading be *RMP Cyprus Veterans' Group* or should it be *Veteran's Group*. Or should there be no apostrophe at all?

I favour the … *Veterans' Group* as the group belongs to the veterans, but this is being challenged.

A: Unless the whole event is being organised for just one veteran, then you are correct. *RMP Cyprus Veterans' Group.*

Q: Would the following statement be correct?

The Company's trucks' international journeys' statistics are constantly considered.

I am currently correcting a document for a client (I'm Russian, so we're going Russian to English here) and without using the word 'of' a lot, this sentence is just absolutely awful. How would you say this in beautiful English?

A: Statistics from our trucks' international journeys are constantly considered.
Constant consideration is given to the statistics from the company's trucks' international journeys.
International journey statistics from the company's trucks are constantly considered.

© Ruth Hartnup

Q: In the sentence *there are 3 ds in Daddy* should it be *ds* or *d's*?

A: The problem arises because 'd' is not a word. To be consistent and follow the rule, is should be *ds* but that doesn't read well. To make the point that the 's' signifies more that one 'd', try using upper case, as in
there are 3 Ds in Daddy.

Q: Please clarify if an apostrophe is needed at the end of the following sentence:

David is a lawyer for Wellington, Marlborough, Waikato and Far North Councils.

Thanks

A: None needed. Councils is simply a plural.

,

Q: I administer an annual awards scheme for our volunteers. Each year the runners up receive a book each as recognition. Our chairman needs to sign these books.

In the sentence *the chairman needs to sign the runners up books* where should the apostrophe and 's' go? Since runner up is pluralised by adding the 's' after the first word (I believe) do I add 's after the word 'up' or just an apostrophe after the word 'runners'?

A: This is an awkward one because it's a combination word. One could hyphenate it to be *runner-up* and I have seen the plural in this case as *runner-ups*. But that sounds awkward as well. *Runners up* is probably the best plural but then one runs into apostrophe problems as you have found. Whichever solution is suggested the result is not good.

How about *the chairman needs to sign the books for the runners up*?

Q: The trophy reads ... *The Past Captains Consolation Plate*. Do I need an apostrophe after the word captain, as it will be a plate belonging to the winning past captain?

A: Basically if there's one captain involved it should be *captain's*. If it's about all past captains, then it should be *captains'*.

When you go outside please turn off:

- The electric city

- The fan, and Lock the door.

Q: When you have a plural acronym do you put an apostrophe before the 's'. By way of example:

The phrase frequently asked questions is often abbreviated to FAQ's

But is it FAQs or FAQ's?

My belief is that it is *FAQ's* as an apostrophe should be used to pluralise an acronym – your missing letter rule would appear to support this as 'Q' is short for questions so letters are missing. However, if that rule was strictly applied surely it would be *F'A'Q's*, which is clearly incorrect.

Incidentally, I believe my understanding about acronyms also applies to numbers, so you would say in the *1960's*, not in the *1960s*, or she is in her early *20's*, not she is in her early *20s*.

A: There is a point at which an acronym becomes a word in itself. Think of Gestapo or Unesco. I think that FAQ has reached that stage. I would therefore opt for *FAQs* without the apostrophe.

I also have a view on dates and numbers. One is simply pluralising so there is no requirement for the apostrophe. I was born in the 1940s and am now in my 60s.

,

Q: How would you use the apostrophes in:

Seniors Captains Honours Board

A: Given that there is more than one senior involved and more than one captain, without further information or knowledge of the context I would suggest

Seniors' Captains' Honours Board.

Honours is simply a plural noun describing the board, so does not require an apostrophe.

Q: I recently overheard a colleague being criticised for not putting an apostrophe in *Parents Evening*. Had they wanted to, they would have written *Parents' Evening*, to show that the evening belonged to or was for the parents; but they wanted to use *Parents* to describe the evening, as in 'What kind of evening?' 'A parents evening!'

Despite trawling through some clear and scholarly articles and discussion pages, I've not found a thorough analysis of the possible adjectival role of plural nouns like parents, veterans, leaders, deacons, ladies. In short, what's the difference between *Parents' Evening* and *Parents Evening*? Can the latter be used to give a sense that the evening is about, for, with parents, but not of them?

A: You are not the first to pose this question and as you have discovered, it is open to question. My personal preference would be to use the apostrophe, as you say it is an evening for parents even if they don't 'own' it in a possessive sense. It is therefore what is known in grammatical terms as an objective genitive. As a genitive, it merits the apostrophe. I know there is an argument that it is adjectival in this case, but it's not one I support.

I note too that you are writing from a school, so if only to keep the pedantic parents at bay, I would suggest using the apostrophe!

,

© Stewart Black

Q: Could you confirm whether there should be any apostrophe at all in the following team title:

Assessments and Interventions Team.

I think there probably shouldn't be any?

A: I think you're right. Without knowing the context, I would suggest they are both plurals rather than possessives. So nothing is missing, so no apostrophes are required.

,

Q: *Partners' meeting.*

I don't think there should be any apostrophe but they are adamant. Can you confirm?

A: This would depend on the context to some extent, but I think it refers to a meeting of the partners. There being more than one partner (and it would be hard to be a solo partner) then the apostrophe should come after the 's'. Partners – partnerses – partners'.

Q: Is an apostrophe needed in the sentence:

One of the commandos fell to the ground.

I'm not sure if I should use one or not.

A: I assume you are thinking whether *commandos* needs an apostrophe. The answer is no. It is a plural, not a contraction or possessive. Nothing is missing so no apostrophe is required.

© Subberculture

Q: *Children's toys*? Why not *Childrens' toys* as in *boys' coats* (assuming there are lots of boys and lots of children ...?)?

ALSO

The book belonging to Cassius is Cassius's book

Why is it not Cassius' book?

A: Because *children* is already the plural of child.

Some (Americans mainly) would argue it should be *Cassius'* book, but if you apply the rule, you get *Cassius's book*. Both are seen (because of American usage) in the main, but my preference is to be consistent, apply the rule and so use *Cassius's*.

Q: Why is there (or was there) an apostrophe in *Hallowe'en* and also why doesn't ANYONE ever put one at the front of words like *plane* as in *aeroplane* and or *phone* as in *telephone*?

A: All Hallows Eve = Hallowevening = Hallowe'en. Because after much usage they are now accepted as words in their own right. Language is constantly evolving and changing if in daily use. English is not frozen like Latin, for example.

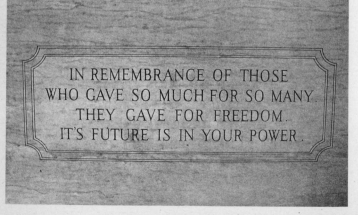

IN REMEMBRANCE OF THOSE
WHO GAVE SO MUCH FOR SO MANY.
THEY GAVE FOR FREEDOM.
IT'S FUTURE IS IN YOUR POWER.

© Sylvar

Q: the *agentes* telephone
the *agent's* telephone
one agent, one phone

the *agentses* telephone
the *agents'* telephone
more than one agent, just one phone

the *agentses* telephones
the *agents'* telephones
can this mean:
1. There is more than one agent and each has a telephone
and
2. there is more than one agent and each has more than one telephone?

How to make the distinction between 1 and 2 has always baffled me.

A: You can't simply by using apostrophes. They deal only with the possessive nouns, in this case *agents'* but not the thing that is possessed, such as the telephones. If it is important to clarify how many phones each agent has, then the sentence would need to be rewritten to show that.

Q: My boss has produced a piece of promotional material for an event and has put the title as:

What Get's Measured Get's Done.

I think this is wrong — surely? There is nothing missing (you wouldn't say *what get is measured get is done*) and nothing belongs to anything ... so it's not possessive.

I told her this with complete conviction and now it's being questioned and I've lost my conviction! Please confirm.

A: I confirm. You are absolutely right. No apostrophes needed.

The REAL ESTATE CLUB

You Don't Wan't The Competition

To Catch Up.

Paddle Faster! Join the REC at one of its semester meet and greets to learn more about the club. The meet and greets are January 27th 12-1pm or January 28th 7-8pm in the Manners room, 7th floor RCB.

In case of burning need to talk to us or standard question please feel free to reach us at ~~kxxxxx@xxxxx.xxx~~ (REC)

© Sylvar

© William Murphy

Q: What is the proper way to use an apostrophe at the start of a sentence? For instance:

('*Cause* or '*cause*) I said so.
('*Ello* or '*ello*), luv.
('*Ow* or '*ow*) 're you doing?
('*Til* or '*til*) the cows come home.

Thanks.

A: Interesting, and you are the first person to raise this. One can argue that the first letter should be lower case because the initial upper-case letter is replaced by the apostrophe. Technically that may be correct, but upon reflection I think it would be better to use an upper-case letter as in the first of each of your examples. It just looks better.

,

Q: Do you by any chance know the rule for 'etc.'? Microsoft Word insists there should not be two full stops after it at the end of a sentence, but surely two makes sense?! Thanks for any help.

A: For once, Word is right. A full stop is a full stop. It stops the sentence as well as ending the abbreviation. You can only kill something once!

Q: Is the use of the apostrophe in the following sentence correct?

Appendix D also contains details of my firms' current charging and disbursements policy.

Or should it be ... *firm's current charging ...* ?

I would have thought the latter. Your help would be appreciated greatly.

A: It depends how many firms you have.

If you have several firms, then it's *firms'*.
If you have one firm, then it's *firm's*.

The section about the coats and the boys applies here. This is why it can be so important to place the dreaded apostrophe correctly.

© Jeremy Keith

Q: *Systems Manager*
or
Systems' Manager

Please could you clarify.

A: This all depends on how it is interpreted. If one regards the term as possessive, that is a manager of systems, then *Systems' Manager* would be appropriate. Unless of course the manager manages only one system, in which case *System's Manager* would be correct.

However, if one regards the term as descriptive, that is simply describing the type of manager, then *Systems Manager* could be used.

I think the last is the more common, but whichever you decide to use at least now you can justify it to critics.

,

Q: I hope you can settle an argument we are having. Is it *'The leaver's assembly'* or *'the leavers' assembly'* when there is more than one leaver?

A: There's no reason to have an argument! Simply apply the rule. Given that this involves more than one leaver as you say, then you start with the plural *leavers*. Add the *es* to show possession = *leaverses* and then omit the possessive ending = *leavers'*.

,

Q: Should I have an apostrophe in *students' names* when I mean to say 'the names of the students'? It does seem to fit in the pretend Chaucer *studentses names*. Am I correct? If so, I seem to have gotten the single rule 'when letters are missing'.

What about *course results* meaning 'results of the course? Why not use apostrophe?

A: You are correct *students' names* is the correct use of the apostrophe there.

Results is simply a plural – nothing 'belongs' to the results, they belong to the course. You might consider *course's results* for one course, or *courses' results* for the results from several courses. But it is usually expressed as a double noun, that is *course* is part of a single expression. One of those things in a dynamic language.

,

Q: Which is the correct one:
doll's house
or
dolls house?

dolls' house
or
doll house?

I understand that it should be doll house as compared to brick house, dog house, etc. What does *dolls' house* mean?

It is all confusing to me: *doll house, dolls house*; *doll's house, dolls' house*. I would appreciate your explanation on this.

A: It's a house for dolls, so I favour *dolls' house*. The analogy with brick house would only be valid if the house was made of dolls!

Q: Please could you help me with a question that one of my students asked me? Would *Bachelors Degree* or *Honours Degree* have an apostrophe? I would so appreciate your input.

A: I would think not. This is because they are adjectives describing the type of degree. In fact, I would suggest that *bachelor degree* is more accurate than with the 's'. In the case of a degree with honours, again, *Honours* is a plural noun, being used to describe the degree.

Q: Singular nouns ending with 's' do not require any special treatment when it comes to an apostrophe usage for their possessive forms. However, I have seen that American English likes to omit the second 's'. Would you say both are correct then? *James's books* and *James' books* (*Alex's ideas* or *Alex' ideas*).

Many thanks in advance.

A: *James's* is more consistent and adheres to a single rule. Some American usage omits the second 's' when the name ends in 's'. I prefer the consistent usage.

Alex does not end in 's' so the possessive should always be *Alex's*.

,

Q: We are applying your Chaucer rule to my 9-year-old son's homework and are getting confused over a couple of sentences on where to put the apostrophe. We would be grateful for any help/explanation if you have the time.

1. *5KWs class service is today.*
2. *Year 3s school trip is on Monday.*
3. *Hill Brooks motto is ...*
4. *Mr Williams class is good.*

I think the following is correct. However, I don't want to give the wrong advice and confuse him even more!

1. *5KW's class.*
2. *Year 3's school trip.*
3. *Hill Brook's motto.*
4. *Mr Williams' class.*

A: 1, 2 and 3 are correct.

I would prefer *Mr Williams's* class as it is more consistent. However, proper nouns tend to be a law unto themselves and American usage would not favour the second 's'.

,

9 PERSONS 1000KG
OR
1 HORSE
5,050 BANANAS
6,666 HENS EGGS
2,941 PIGEONS
88 HADDOCK
10,526 POUND COIN

© THP

Q: This is the text: *one of the elders houses*. Where does the apostrophe go here? Before or after the 's' of *elders*?

A: This would entirely depend on whether the reference is to one elder who may own several houses, or lots of elders each with a house. That is why correct placing of the apostrophe is important: its position can radically alter the meaning.

CHILDREN AND OTHER PLURAL NOUNS

When a noun is already plural, meaning there is more than one of whatever it is, puzzlement sets in. This is even worse because the plural usually ends in an 's', and that final 's' causes confusion. I hope the following Q&As will help clarify this for the reader.

Q: Is it correct to write:

Patients that get Athena/Genetic Testing will most likely not be covered by their insurance companies.

or should I write:

Patient's that get Athena/Genetic Testing will most likely not be covered by their insurance companies.

A: The first is correct:

Patients that get Athena/Genetic Testing will most likely not be covered by their insurance companies.

It is simply a plural noun, not possessive.

Q: *Kid's Karnival* or *Kids' Karnival*? (We are spelling carnival with a 'K' because it takes place during a 10K run.)

A: *Kid's* would be correct if it were a carnival for just one kid! Unlikely. So you start with the plural *Kids* because you have lots of them.

Pretend Chaucer = *Kidses*. Modern usage = *Kids'*.

Q: Please help: which of the following is correct? She should try to show how religion affects *people's lives* OR *peoples' lives*.

A: Here you are using *people* as a plural noun, so the analogy would be with *children* already a plural noun. So in this case *people's lives* is correct.

People can sometimes be used as a singular noun and then made plural, e.g. *peoples of the world*, etc. If one wished to show possession in that case, applying the rule to a plural noun would render *peoples'*.

FREQUENTLY ASKED QUESTIONS

Q: I have a query on a word that is bugging me ...

Kids

Obviously, *kid's* means the one child's – *The kid's bike was green* – the one child has a green bike. *The kids' all wore green coats* – all of the children, plural, had green coats.

But when would I use *kids* without any apostrophe, and what would this mean? Thanks so much in advance for your help!

A: In your example, *The kids all wore green coats*, no apostrophe is required. It is simply the plural of *kid*. After all, would you write, *The children's all wore green coats*? No, it's simply, *The children all wore green coats*. The plural of *child*.

Q: My daughter received homework which she needed to proofread and correct, and it read as:

Everyone's knees

Should it be *Everyones' knees* as it is a posses-sive plural?

A: Common sense tells you that *everyone* is plural because it means lots of people. But, in fact, the clue is in the *one* part and it is singular, as *every one*. One says 'Everyone is going to the ball', not 'Everyone are going to the ball.'

So in fact your daughter was correct, as is *Everyone's knees.*

,

Q: I am struggling to understand how to use apostrophes, particularly when possessives are concerned.

The title of my dissertation is:

Opinions on using Facebook as a Method of Communication between YOT Practitioners and Young Offenders

I have no idea whether *YOT Practitioners* should have an apostrophe or *Young Offenders* should have one? I'm guessing *Opinions* doesn't need one.

I have a number of graphs and where my titles state *young offenders opinions on* ... again I don't know where the apostrophe goes.

A: The title does not require any apostrophes because they are all plural nouns. In your graph titles, the apostrophe is required because they are the opinions of a young offender, or of several young offenders. Assuming we are talking about several, then it should come after the word offenders, so *young offenders' opinions*.

,

Q: I would be grateful if you would cast some light on the following play title:

An evening with the Ponsonby-Smythe's
or
An evening with the Ponsonby-Smythes

I believe it is correct in the latter since it is plural. Would you like to confirm one way or the other? I am producing a poster to advertise the play.

A: You are right, the latter is correct. It is simply a plural.

Q: Can you tell me what is correct here please *Ladies Festival* or *Ladies' Festival*:

After dinner at the Ladies festival we will sing the Ladies Song (or Ladies' Song).

Many thanks

A: It's a festival for ladies and a song for ladies. Ladies is already a plural noun so following the 'Chaucer' rule, you end up with *Ladies' Festival where after dinner you will sing the Ladies' Song.*

Q: Does this phrase need an apostrophe?

I need access to the companies own data.

A: One company or several? If it's one company then the correct version is:

I need access to the company's own data.

If several companies, then it's:

I need access to the companies' own data.

© THP

PLACE NAMES

Place names are awkward, there's no doubt about it. Even more if the place name ends in an 's'. I hope the advice given here to others is useful to the reader.

Q: Can I ask you whether you write Paris's or Paris' when we say:

Working in Paris'(s) famous hotel ?

A: Paris's. It's also how one says it. The part of the **Possessives** section about The Book of Cassius explains this.

Q: Just an inquiry. Is the street name *King's Road* correct with the apostrophe in?
Many thanks.

A: Assuming that, like most, it was named for one king in particular at that time, then yes, it's correct.

Q: I run a small B&B by the sea in Bude, North Cornwall. As the only B&B in Bude by the sea, am I ...

Bude's only B&B by the sea
or
Budes' only B&B by the sea ?

Or is there no apostrophe at all?

A: The first one is correct. There's only one Bude!

Q: Hello. I live in a small country town that has a large river running through it and many creeks that flow into the river. The river was named after a man called Page and two creeks were named after men called Boyd and Single. Throughout history they were referred to as the Page River, the River Page or the Page's River. Same with Boyd's Creek and Single's Creek. The Geographical Names Board has done away with the apostrophe and they are now officially known as Pages River, Boyds Creek and Singles Creek (the spell check incidentally tries to correct Boyds). I find this wrong and discourteous to the men they were named after as it effectively changes their names. They were not Mr Pages or Mr Boyds or Mr Singles. I emailed the GNB to ask them why they have left out the apostrophe and their reply was:

'The Geographical Names Board (the Board) decided that the possessive form should be avoided whenever possible without destroying the name or changing its descriptive application. Therefore geographical names such as Boyds Creek now have the apostrophe left out.'

Maybe you can shed some light on this?

A: The US dropped such punctuation in 1890 when the US Board of Geographic Names removed the apostrophe from its database. Only five exceptions have ever been made, including Martha's Vineyard, Massachusetts, in 1933. Australia followed suit in 2001 for the sake of consistency in the databases used by the emergency services.

In Birmingham in the UK last year the council decided to drop apostrophes in place names and there was an outcry but the bureaucrats stuck to their guns. But it survives in some other British place names.

TIME

It can often be difficult to decide whether words indicating time are being used in a possessive/genitive sense or as adjectives/descriptors. This is perhaps the thorniest area of dispute as to whether to use and apostrophe or not, and of so, where it should be placed.

In the Q&As below, I have tried to answer each case as it came along based on the information and context I was provided with. In each case I have tried to apply the system as consistently as I could.

,

Q: I would be extremely grateful if you would settle an argument that is raging in the office amongst people who really should know better (they are experts in intellectual property!)

The argument refers to the period that must be given before a change can be introduced. Is it:

(a) *X will give at least 3 months notice ...*
(b) *X will give at least 3 month's notice ...*

(c) *X will give at least 3 months' notice ...*

A: The question is really whether *months* in this case is a noun 'possessing' the notice or an adjective describing the notice.

If one regards it as a possessing noun, then the answer lies in the section concerning possessives. The word *months* here is a plural (more than one month) so it follows the same track as *boys coats* on that page:

Pretend Chaucer = 3 monthses notice
Modern correct form = 3 months' notice
The 'es' is replaced by the apostrophe.

One could argue that *months* here is used to describe the length of notice required and, although a noun, is in this context de facto an adjective, and therefore requires no apostrophe as nothing is missing, case (a) above.

As we derive this from the Germanic roots of English, it seems sensible to have some regard to the German. It is clear from that usage that months (*Monate*) is used as a descriptor and is not a genitive case. It also seems more logical, as a month cannot 'own' the notice, so I therefore prefer *(a) X will give at least 3 months notice* ... Nonetheless, it is most common to use the apostrophe.

,

Q: Could you please help me? I read a notice at our local club which stated:

The club will remain open all day Saturday's.

When I pointed out that Saturdays does not have an apostrophe, I was shot down in flames in a very rude way.

A: You are right. But actually the final 's' isn't really needed anyway:

The club will remain open all day on Saturday.
or
The club will remain open all day every Saturday.

would be even better.

Q: Can you settle a dispute over *New Year's Eve*? I think *Year's* should have an apostrophe as placed but my client is not so sure and thinks they will have complaints. There is an 'e' missing?

A: I'm with you – it should have one. It is the eve of the New Year even it doesn't own it in a possessive sense. It is therefore what is known in grammatical terms as an objective genitive. As a genitive, it merits the apostrophe.

Q: Can you please clear up the following queries and advise me which is the correct answer?

1.
(a) Some of our managers enjoy 30 days' annual leave per year.
or
(b) Should managers' enjoy 30 days annual leave per year.

2.
(a) Britain's most famous kings' and queens'.
or
(b) Britain's most famous kings and queens.

I would be grateful if you could please clarify.

A: In number 1, neither (a) nor (b) require any apostrophe. *Days* is a plural and so is *managers*.
    In number 2, the only possessive is *Britain's*. So (b) is correct.

Q: What is the correct use of apostrophe in the scenario below?

Season's Greetings from Rob

Is this correct?

A: I think you are correct, but it is not often seen.

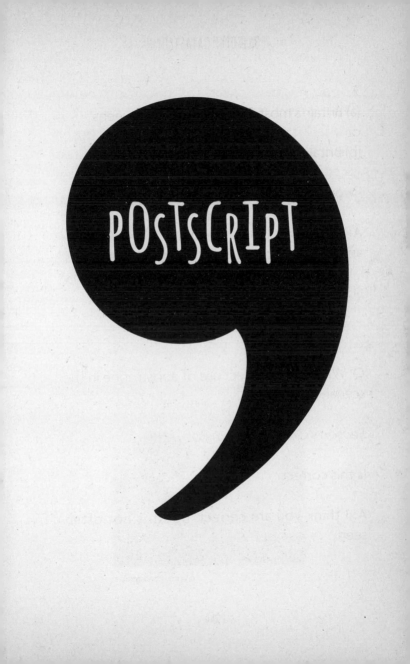

I hope you have found this book both entertaining and enlightening. Once a book is printed it is set, perhaps not in stone but in paper and ink. The website that inspired this book will continue to evolve and readers are more than welcome to send comments about the single-rule system and, as many have done before, send questions. I will do my best to answer. I look forward to hearing from you at www.dreaded-apostrophe.com.

© www.broadsheet.ie